SYSTEM OF EXECUTION
KEEPING RIGHT PERFORMANCE ON-TRACK
CHIN TEIK

VISION BHAG
- STRATEGIES ACHIEVED
- ANNUAL TARGETS MET

KEPPING RIGHT PERFORMACE ON TRACK
- DISCIPLINED LEADERSHIP
- BREAKTHROUGH PERFORMANCE
- CULTURE OF EXECUTION

CLARITY FOR FOCUSED EXECUTION
- ROLE
- GAPS
- BARRIERS

1-PAGE CONSTANCY OF PURPOSE
- WHY
- WHERE
- HOW
- WHAT

A HOW-TO BOOK
OBTAIN COMMITMENT TO EXECUTE

SYSTEM of EXECUTION

Keeping Right Performance On-Track

Copyright © 2025 Cheah Chin Teik

All rights reserved. No part of this book may be reproduced, stored in a retrieval system, distributed, or transmitted in any form or any means, including photocopying, recording or any other electronic or mechanical methods, without the prior written permission of the author, except in the case of brief quotations embodied in critical reviews, and certain other noncommercial uses permitted by copyright law.

For Emilia Cheah

MY WISH

Thank you for the purchase of this how-to book tool kit. It is meant to be used: write on it, fill up the templates/toolkits, frameworks, underscore keywords or phrases, and make notes on the cross-reference with other books. **Generation** (neuroscience) is when an individual is motivated to understand, contextualize, retain, and apply knowledge in their own way; personalize it by transforming it in a way that is meaningful to them. That is ownership of learning.

This how-to book toolkit is written in the spirit of action learning: learn by doing, apply via the toolkits templates/frameworks that I have designed. Take the time to press the 'pause button' and reflect to generate for insight. I have also included my podcasts to support your learning. Please check out my podcast channel: Up-Close with Chin Teik: Re-Think

This how-to book tool kit is also designed to be interactive with the author, me. You can reach me at chin.teik@chinteik.com or www.linkedin.com/in/chin-teik-cheah-201b096 if you have questions, reactions, insights, or interests in with the topic tools provided.

CHIN TEIK CONSULTING LTD

FOREWORD

Chin Teik brings a wealth of real-world experience and a lifetime of coaching to this insightful book, offering pragmatic advice that leaders can apply daily.

The models he presents provide leaders with a framework to translate vision into focused execution. While this may sound simple, it often fails due to an organization's inherent resistance to change and individuals' attempts to control the uncontrollable. His solution emphasizes spending more time identifying the right problems, engaging key stakeholders, and developing both intrinsic lead and lagging indicators. Success hinges on disciplined leadership, consistent feedback, situational adaptability, and a culture of execution. This comprehensive book covers it all and, if followed, promises breakthrough performance through clear focus and accountability.

Colin Browne

CEO

Cascale

When I first encountered the work of Chin Teik, I was immediately struck by the clarity and precision with which he addressed one of the most pervasive challenges facing modern businesses—execution. His insights resonated deeply with my own experiences in leading retail brands across the globe. Like many leaders, I've seen first-hand that even the most brilliant strategies, without disciplined execution, rarely achieve their full potential.

This book, "Keeping Right Performance on Track," offers not only a framework for execution but a disciplined approach that goes beyond the theoretical. Chin Teik has laid out a system that every leader, whether in retail or any other industry, should adopt. As Bill Gates aptly put it, "The most brilliant strategy won't lead to success, unless executed well."

Having had the privilege of leading retail initiatives for brands like New Balance and Adidas, I can attest to the importance of keeping performance on track, as Chin Teik so aptly describes. The balance between planning and execution is often skewed, with many organizations dedicating significant time to creating the perfect strategy but far less to the rigor of execution. Chin Teik's emphasis on the culture of execution and disciplined leadership is what sets this book apart. In my own journey, I've seen remarkable growth when these principles are applied. This success was not due to strategy alone, but the focused execution of the right priorities across every facet of the business. As Steve Jobs said, "To me, ideas are worth nothing unless executed. They are just a multiplier. Execution is worth millions."

The toolkit that Chin Teik provides in this book isn't just theory; it's grounded in real-world application. His approach, with its emphasis on disciplined leadership and individual breakthrough performance, has guided me in delivering innovative retail strategies and customer experiences, often in the most challenging of market conditions.

For those who, like me, are passionate about driving growth, enhancing brand equity, and delivering tangible results, "Keeping Performance on Track" offers the blueprint to move from mere strategy to measurable success. This book is a must-read for anyone committed to leading their organization towards a future where execution, not just vision, is the true differentiator.

Bob Neville

Strategic Global Retail Leader

As a fellow Malaysian, I would like to congratulate Chin Teik on the publication of his book – 'Keeping Right Performance on Track'. Given my experience of working with Chin Teik on leadership development and senior executive coaching, I know that Chin Teik brings a wealth of experience and exposure into his framework and toolkits as well as the delivery and multiplier impact on the people he works with.

His work on the System of Execution, especially Keeping Right Performance on Track, is timely as I believe that the ROI in all the strategic planning is in the execution of the prioritized strategies to achieve the business results. The rhythm of accountability is an important part of an organization culture to deliver consistent results to the shareholders.

I highly recommend this book if you are interested in moving from plan to commit to plan to execute.

Dato K.C. Gan

Chairman,

The Malaysian Chamber of Commerce, Hong Kong & Macau

It has been an enlightening experience going through what Chin Teik has brought together in this toolkit. Both strategy and execution is important and symbiotic for an organisation to be successful - that is why it is imperative that strategic thinking be coupled with strategic planning, which helps translate strategy to plans of execution. Even as our organisation is undergoing a reset in terms of execution excellence, I can already see a vision of which we are better off at delivering what we promised, year after year.

For those who would like to move from commitment to plan to commitment to execute, I recommend getting a copy of Chin Teik's Keeping Right Performance on Track.

Aaron Chin

COO

New Hoong Fatt Group

Learning is Recall & Change in Behavior

L — **Learning** starts with knowing what you don't know and/or what you would like to solve. Begin by asking what you are trying to solve or achieve.

E — **Engage** the book toolkit by using the templates, answering the questions; write on the book not on a separate piece of paper or notebook for easy retrieval

A — **Accountability** for your own learning; there will be no one chasing you and asking you to read a chapter or do your homework

R — **Relate** the concepts and process to yourself, your group of stakeholders. Generation is for insight, which leads to action and change.

N — **No judgment** on concepts and process until you have tried them. If you do not empty your cup of tea, you will not be able to taste my cup of tea. A cup's usefulness is in its emptiness.

The key to learning is **RECALL** and **(APPLICATION) BEHAVIOR CHANGE**. The first step is sometimes the most difficult but most important in any learning: willingness to try something new while **feeling uncomfortable**.

Mastery over any skill requires **deliberate**, **disciplined practice** over a sustained period of time ~ Chin Teik

Warm-Up Questions

1. How do you rate your organization's focused execution of plans to right priorities consistently?
    - ❏ 100%
    - ❏ 50 to 90%
    - ❏ Below 50%

2. How do you keep the right performance on track?

3. What are your three barriers to 100% focused execution?

4. Rate accountability level of self and others?

    - ❏ 100%
    - ❏ 80%
    - ❏ 50% and below

5. What are the three barriers to 100% accountability at an individual level?

Importance of Reflection: AGES for Recall & Change

Learning occurs when there is **insight** leading to behavior change. Knowledge, if not used over a certain period of time, will get lost. Moving knowledge from short-term memory to long-term memory requires connecting current and new knowledge to the application of knowledge — recalling the knowledge instantly and over a certain period of time under pressure.

Reflection is one of the key aspects of experiential learning. **AGES** is the neuroscience of brain-friendly learning — **Attention, Generation, Emotion, and Spacing.**
https://resultscoaches.co.za/wp-content/uploads/2015/05/ages.pdf

Experiential learning is learning by doing and taking time to reflect on the key learning that comes with the doing. Not all things can be taught and even if taught may not be internalized by the individual. So experiential learning is not optimized without reflection time on the action for insights.

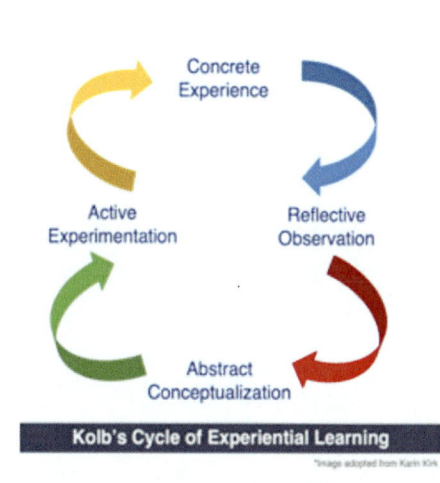

Kolb's Cycle of Experiential Learning

- Concrete Experience
- Reflective Observation
- Abstract Conceptualization
- Active Experimentation

Image adopted from Karin Kirk

Note on Kolb's Cycle of Experiential Learning

David Kolb is professor of organizational behavior in Weatheread School of Management.

He has been awarded four honorary degrees for his contribution to experiential learning. David A. Kolb (with Roger Fry) created his famous model out of four elements: concrete experience, observation and reflection, the formation of abstract concepts and testing in new situations.

Kolb and Fry (1975) argue that the learning cycle can begin at any one of the four points – and that it should really be approached as a continuous spiral.

Learning Journal Reflection For Insights:

I developed this reflection tool (developed over many years of working with individuals and teams in experiential learning mode) to facilitate the transition from experience to reflection to internalization, generation to insight and to action.

In my previous working life in a global company, I would set aside time in a week — meeting with myself — for reflection and planning. It is a process to 'press the pause button' and take the time to reflect, think and plan for actions based on insights.

Reflection for Insights (Aha!)

Observations, new concepts: **Knowing**

Anytime during the learning process, you come across a new concept, an old concept revisited, or an observation about yourself or your team member, write it down in this column.

#Pause #Language #Re-Think   **Re-Framing**

Reflect on the new #language you are coming across.

- ➤ #Pause to not judge, to not accept the new #language
- ➤ #Pause to re-look at your current frame of mind reflected in your language
- ➤ #Pause to answer "How does the new #language make me better?"

How does this apply to ME, my-TEAM and my-GROUP? Being

Reflect as to how you can apply the observation and new concepts you came across during the workshop learning. **Relevance.**

- ➤ First, what is the reason and the result that can achieved if you are to apply the concept or insights to yourself personally?
- ➤ Secondly, how can you apply the same concept or insights to your team?

➤ Thirdly, how can you apply the same concept or insights to your group (personal workgroups as well)?

Actions to MYSELF: Doing

If there are applications that can be used to either yourself, your team or your group, then write down what you are going to do specifically and by when (a specific date is recommended).

To ensure the integrity of actions, recommend that you set specific actions and deadlines for completion of actions.

An even more powerful impact is public accountability – to share with someone what you are going to do differently in terms of a new habit after the learning.

'Insight, I believe, refers to the process by which a shift in perspective reveals a coherent pattern that had previously been obscured from view." – Mary Catherine Bateson

Reflection for Insights (Aha!)

Observations, New Concepts Aha!	How does this apply to ME, my-TEAM & my-GROUP?	Actions to MYSELF What, Why, When, How

Action Learning Objectives

➢ **Apply first 3 of 6 Self-to-Development with regards to:**

- System of Execution: Keeping Right Performance on Track: 1 requirement & 2 elements
- Role of Situational Leader-Manager: 4 Styles, 2-Rhythm & 2 Rules of Feedback
- Capability to apply the tools up to 70%
- Agree on organization's Culture of Execution
- Able to recall under pressure over one week, one month, and three months

➢ **Begin a Self-Development Plan to move to "being"**
- Knowing-**Being**-Doing

➢ **Learn principles and framework by 'doing'**
- Application and social learning

6 Steps Self-to-Development

We are limited by our current paradigm of self from our **4E** – environment, education, experience, exposure - and unconscious biases.

Development cannot begin without being first aware that you have a gap to close between the current state and the future state. That self-awareness can only occur when you are **open** (**mindset**) to a standard or a future state of being a better self, which you believe can be attained through dedication and hard work — a **growth mindset**.

SELF	COMPETENCE	
Awareness	Unconscious Incompetency to Conscious Incompetency	
Honest		
Assessment		Novice
Development	Conscious Competency to Unconscious Competency	Experienced Beginner
Accountability		Practitioner
Refresh		Expert

"Possibility is Limited by Our Current Paradigm" ~ Chin Teik

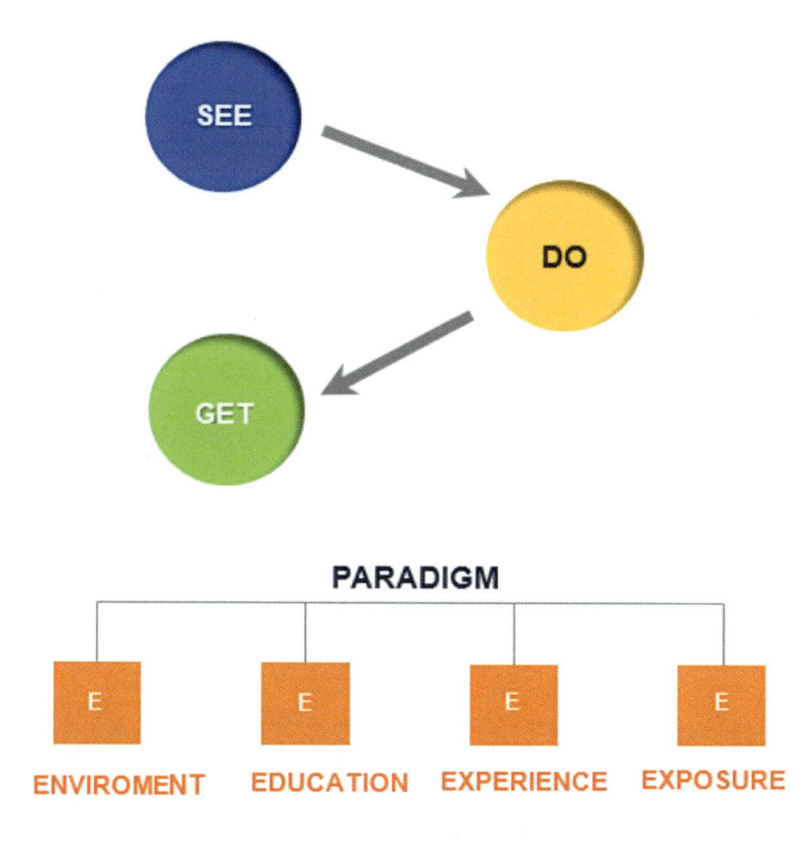

```
     SEE
       ↘
         DO
        ↙
     GET
```

PARADIGM

E	E	E	E
ENVIROMENT	EDUCATION	EXPERIENCE	EXPOSURE

Re-Frame _____, **"Do"** and **"Get"** will become different.

Possibility is Limited by Our Current Paradigm

https://open.spotify.com/episode/0BLGPtDj4ZrJB949oLdM1t?si=B0saiRFMSkS_IDYBwB40rA&context=spotify%3Ashow%3A0qewTFcM3EZIQOD9Lw89JK

FRAMEWORK

KEEPING RIGHT PERFORMANCE ON TRACK

Key Point: Organizational Leaders and Managers Need to Balance Between Commitment to Plan and Commitment to Execute

Keeping Right Performance on Track - An Overview

https://open.spotify.com/episode/4iAjMDNCuUowiYRKbpOoUi?si=9kFdrn-wQqCNT4BbSqPDHg

Keeping Right Performance on Track: System of Execution

The key to focused execution is clarity and discipline requiring:
- Clear role expectations
- Focus on leading indicators rather than lag outcomes
- Using the 20/80 Rule for focused impact
- Accountability with clear consequences at an individual level

It is easier to set goals than to achieve the goals. We are often our own worst enemy due to:
- Emotional defaults of overwhelm and frustration
- Losing motivation (Will) as it takes too long
- Our SEEDS (unconscious bias) have us use the existing Way (How) to achieve new goals
- Our inability to stay focused while continuing to say yes to new tasks

System of Execution
Keeping Right Performance on Track
Obtaining Commitment To Execute

1 Requirement	Element 1	Element 2
Disciplined Leadership	**Individual Breakthrough Performance**	**Culture of Execution**
Applying PHS with 2 Rules of Feedback o Priority o Habit o System	1. Executing on Leading Indicators to Achieve Lag Outcomes Expectations 2. Visual Self-Monitoring Performance Feedback – lead 3. Control of Resources	Success Mindset o Growth o Open o Outward o Promotion
Situational Leader-Manager o Supportive behaviour o Directive behaviour 2-Rhythm o Relationship o Accountability Lead-by-example on o Breakthrough Performance o Culture of Execution		Prioritized Practices o Critical Thinking o Structured Problem Solving & Decision-Making o Stakeholder Engagement & Communicating for Impact o High Performing Teams o Lead Change & Manage Transition o Two Rules of Feedback o Issue Clearing o Talent Engagement Habits

The most brilliant strategy won't lead to success unless it's executed effectively

~ Bill Gates

Reflection for Insights (Aha!)

Observations, New Concepts Aha!	How does this apply to ME, my-TEAM & my-GROUP?	Actions to MYSELF What, When, How, Why

PROLOGUE

NEUROSCIENCE OF CHANGE

Key Point: Change Is Required When Closing Gaps Between The Current And The Desired State

Change and Transition Management – An Introduction

https://youtu.be/S6UivAF8r28

https://open.spotify.com/episode/2wGSTeC0ZjTIenqQP2RtVn?si=gB76EN0QReyTVZePB0yyKw&context=spotify%3Ashow%3A0qewTFcM3EZIQOD9Lw89JK

Scalable Change

Change is never easy, even with consequences.

Change is done unto us. Change is quite often immediate and sometimes unplanned and unforeseen.

The reason why change takes so long is because of the emotional transition we go through when impacted by change.

The fear people have with change is the **unknown** that comes with it impacting SCARF.

Questions asked explicitly and implicitly with organization change:
- "Why change now when things are fine?"
- "What will happen to my role with this change? Who will be my new manager?"
- "How long will this change last?"
- "Is this change for real, or will it be another idea that will go away?"
- "This is extra work for me" – "Why do I have to be on this project?"

The brain's goal is to **maximize reward and minimize threat**. The 5 areas where the brain will either experience reward or threat with change — **SCARF** (introduced by Dr. David Rock, 2008).

SCARF

Status	How is an individual's self-worth impacted by the change?
Certainty	Change is always associated with the unknown. What does the future state look like and how is it better?
Autonomy	Does the individual have a choice to go on this journey of change?
Relatedness	Do the impacted people feel safe, psychologically and physically? Is there enough trust to go on the journey of change with the leader or manager?
Fairness	Do the impacted people feel they have been fairly treated? Is the workload fair?

PHS

For scalable change, use PHS (source: Neuroleadership Institute)

Priority	Leadership to communicate the priority for change by using 5R (Reason, Result, Role, Roadmap, Resource)
Habit	Identify 1 habit for change for 30 days throughout the organization
	Important for the leader to be a role model by asking for and acting on the new habit
System	Ensure the system is in place to:
	reinforce the new habit and extinguish the old habit
	help with the 3 stages of emotional transition

Key Point: Change is required for all Projects!

Iceberg Model – Showing Change is Not Easy!

Actions		Visible
#1 Identify prioritised gaps	**EVENTS** — What Just Happened?	Symptom
Understand & Anticipate #2 Current situation analysis	**PATTERNS, TRENDS** over time	Often visible
Redesign with organization design principles #3 Root cause analysis	**SYSTEMIC STRUCTURE** Causal-Effect Relationships	Unaware — Root cause
Unfreeze – Change – Refreeze Manage Emotional Transition #4 Design system solution	**MENTAL MODELS** Paradigms (4E) Assumptions, Beliefs and Values People Hold About the System?	Hidden — Root cause

Freeze mode: People are often stuck in their current state, unknowing/asleep and comfortable – organizational inertia.

People are not ready need to let go of old habits, processes, and structures.

Unfreeze phase: To create a vision of a compelling future state or an option-of-better to awaken people to possibilities. To awaken mindset by challenging assumptions, beliefs, and values of leaders and managers.

Change phase: To implement **System Solution**, experiment, measure, and learn, including organization structures, work processes, and habits. Always begin with the top leaders.

Refreeze: Solidifying the change so that people cannot go back to old habits. Continue to monitor and extinguish old habits.

PRACTICE ONE

5R & 5C

MANAGE SCARF

5R to Communicate Change

https://open.spotify.com/episode/0CjV0i4B43PLi14FaR5e5r?si=gUepXehPTfOL7agxKVyCuQ

5C for Managing Transition

https://open.spotify.com/episode/4Dc6bI9N2j4HCWF7Z84eK3?si=iq9RzHLHSP6sqgGYEYHo1A

5R: Communicating Change

5R - A skill to communicate the change to reduce the threat to SCARF

- Reason
- Results
- Roles
- Roadmap
- Resources

This 5R structure clarifies the unknown to reduce the uncertainty, unnecessary speculation and the negative emotions when threat is experienced in the brain.

FEAR = False Evidence Appearing Real

REASON	People need to know reason for the need for change. Address the 'what's in it for me' to change. Make the message relevant to the respective employees.
RESULTS	SMARTS is one way to communicate results. It depends on whether it is survival, competitive advantage or growth. "What's in it for me to change?"
ROLES	How will the roles change if any for the individuals? **"How will I be impacted?"**
ROADMAP	Duration - start and end dates - of change. **"How long will this last?"** **"How soon before the next change comes?"**
RESOURCES	Who will provide training or development if required; how much time is given? How can I obtain help when I need it? From whom?

> People Don't Fear Change, but the Unknown Associated with Change

Write down the 5R for your proposed change.

REASON	
RESULTS	
ROLES	
ROADMAP	
RESOURCES	

Transition – 3 Emotional Stages

I like the Bridge's transition model because it focuses on transition, not change. Transition is the inner psychological process that people go through as they internalize and come to terms with the new situation that the change brings about.

Transition

- It is internal and happens in people's minds as they experience change
- It usually takes more time and it is different for each individual

Change

- It can happen very quickly and usually without your permission

---

People go through 3 emotional stages during transition per William Bridges' transition model

Bridges' Transition Model

Stage 1 – ending, losing and letting go

Stage 2 – the neutral zone

Stage 3 – the new beginning

Bridges says that each person will go through each stage at their own pace.

There are steps you can take to move through each stage.

You can use the **5C** to identify the transition challenges faced by yourself and others during the change:

Challenge, Control, Connection, Commitment and/or Capability

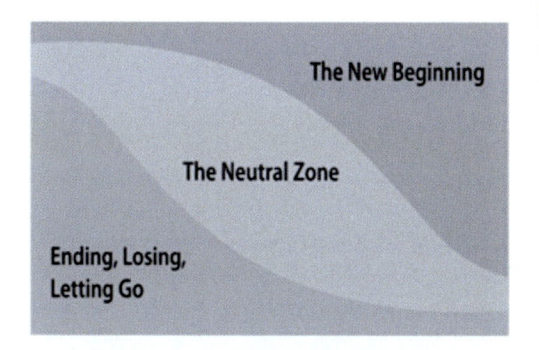

> The starting point for dealing with transition is not the outcome but the endings that people have in leaving the old situation behind.
>
> This first phase of transition begins when people identify what they are losing and learn how to manage these losses.

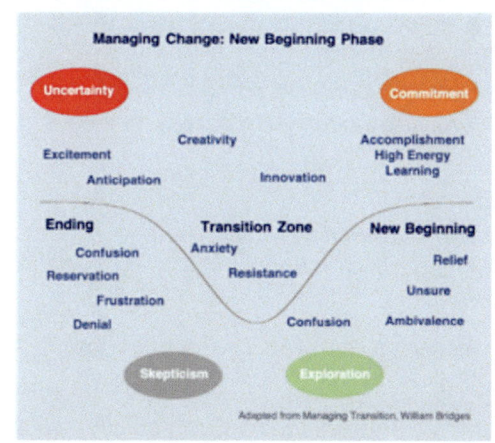

William Bridges an American author, speaker, and consultant.

He emphasized the importance of understanding transitions as a key for organizations to succeed in making changes.

Managing the 5C to Emotional Transition

The **3-Step Change Process** — **Unfreeze-Change-Refreeze** — requires the recognition of the emotional state an individual is in with the perceived or real threat that comes with the change.

The 5C is designed to help with managing SCARF to reduce the feeling of threat and to move to a new beginning.

The ability to assess the combination of C which blocks the unfreezing of the mindset to change.

CHALLENGE	**"Threat or Challenge"** puts the brain into flight or fight mode. The negative aspect of the challenge puts the mindset into a high emotional/low cognitive level and the individual stays in freeze mode.
CONTROL	**"Freaking out or loss of control"** comes from a sense of loss and the threat to the brain with regards to the change.
CONNECTION	**"Loss of identity or connections"** with the perceived role change.
COMMITMENT	**The first 3 C — challenge, control, and connection** will either positively or negatively impact individual's commitment to the change.
CAPABILITY	**Level of commitment** impacts the ability of the individual to learn.

Steps To Managing Transition

Step 1: To identify the people in the organization most impacted by the change your team is proposing.

- Please do not assume that leaders are not impacted — everyone is impacted in one way or another by change
- Different people, due to their paradigms and emotional makeup, have different approaches and reactions to the change

Step 2: To plot where the impacted people are in terms of the 3 stages of transition.

Step 3: To brainstorm on what actions can be taken to help people move through the 3 stages of transition as effectively as possible.

Stage 1	Stage 2	Stage 3	Actions
List names of impacted people	List names of impacted people	List names of impacted people	

Potential Actions to Guide People through the Stages of Transition

Well-managed transitions allow people to establish new roles with an understanding of their purpose, the part they play, and how to contribute and participate most effectively. As a result, they feel reoriented and renewed.

Stage 1: Time of resistance and emotional upheaval

- Provide individual air time to listen to understand each person's emotions
- Take time to explain the 5R so that the emotions are not based on speculations
- Provide time to transition (if possible, based on business conditions)
- Assure that resources will be provided with necessary training or development

Stage 2: Time of uncertainty, confusion, impatience, creativity, innovation and renewal

- Encourage people to try new ways of thinking and working – be patient
- Meet with people to give frequent feedback
- Celebrate quick small wins
- Be aware of extra work load during the transition; help to de-prioritize unimportant tasks

Stage 3: Time of acceptance and high energy

- Link individual's goals to the organization's goals
- Communicate success stories to bigger organization
- Celebrate

Reflection for Insights (Aha!)

Observations, New Concepts Aha!	How does this apply to ME, my-TEAM & my-GROUP?	Actions to MYSELF What, When, How, Why

ONE REQUIREMENT

DISCIPLINED LEADERSHIP

Disciplined Leadership

https://open.spotify.com/episode/7IH7IvmqgRcJtXmc59yhNs?si=Gx5UEVXAR_S0oyWuD5rJ7Q

Disciplined Leadership

Execution requires a discipline of habits and system. Habit is a routine of behavior that is repeated regularly and tends to occur subconsciously. Tony Robbins says: "It's not what we do once in a while that shapes our lives. It's what we do consistently." Thus habit can be formed and habit can be extinguished.

Disciplined leadership is having a rhythm of habits and processes guided by principles. It is the ability to have faith in the process (for example, focus on leading indicators to keep the right performance on track) and demonstrate by example.

Self-discipline is the foundation for disciplined leadership. Here is a simple definition by writer Samuel Thomas Davies "Self-discipline is about leaning into resistance. Taking action in spite of how you feel. Living a lifestyle by design, not by default. But most importantly, it's acting in accordance with your thoughts – not your feelings."

Disciplined leadership is a requirement to visibly scale the organization on breakthrough performance and the culture or habits of execution. It requires the leader-manager to communicate constantly and consistently as well as teach and demonstrate the prioritized habits. They need to have system in place to reinforce and reward the use of prioritized habits.

Disciplined leadership is the one requirement for keeping performance on track. Disciplined leadership is easier said than done. While it sounds simple, it is not easy. It requires a lot of brain effort to not move into default mode. Disciplined leadership requires self-discipline.

Our executive brain (prefrontal cortex) is easily fatigued and defocused (science has shown that multi-tasking does not work). At the same time, people tend to forget that they are humans and behave like robots. This self-fulfilling prophecy is a vicious cycle of in-effectiveness negatively impacting productivity and quality.

Disciplined leadership includes:

- Consistency in words and deeds
- Constancy in Why (Purpose) & How (Strategies)
- Self-control of emotions (temperate)
- Scheduled intentional pauses for self and others to refresh, reflect, and re-think
- Staying true to the process of habits – no shortcuts
    - 2-rhythm – relationship & accountability
    - 2-rules of feedback – positive and advice
- Deprioritizing (the act of subtracting) the non-urgent and non-important to allow the employees to focus

Motivation gets you going, but discipline keeps you growing – John C. Maxwell

A Minute with John Maxwell on Self-Discipline
https://youtu.be/C1tf95V6rhE?si=fwBXUxNmmHd7Xi-E

Tony Robbins: Stay Disciplined
https://youtu.be/-DAgJ_pwkBA?si=RiKFRDxRDB0XWZWk

Jim Collins: Being Great is a Matter of Choice and Discipline
https://youtu.be/nVfqKEM0cmA?si=TEg_pPimc0v3Kxs6

Less is More – Deprioritize (Subtract), a Key Leadership Requirement

A key disciplined leadership requirement for clarity for focused execution is to deprioritize on a regular basis. I call it the rule of subtracting. It is easy to overlook this capability due to the expedient bias and the assumption that the employees' mental and physical capacities are endless. As a result of the unconscious bias and assumption, the employees' plates constantly overflow with great ideas and urgent priorities leading to cognitive overload, physical stress and poor execution.

Two challenges that subtracting helps with:

- Employees (including middle managers) not being able to say 'no' for fear of being viewed as not committed and/or incapable of doing more
- Due to challenge one, managers forget how much is already on the employees' plates and often just add in the name of 'urgency' or 'priority'

Vicious Cycle of Yes

When employees (including middle managers) say yes to everything asked for, the senior management assumes that the employees have limitless mental and physical bandwidth and they keep adding.

The Power of No

"People think focus means yes to the thing you've got to focus on. But that's not what it means at all. It means saying no to the hundreds of good ideas. You have to pick carefully." – Steve Jobs

Saying 'no' with options allows for the pause in the default part of the brain and to re-think priorities as well as the employees' capabilities and mental and physical capacities.

How to Subtract (De-Prioritize)

- Know the why to the how in terms of the vision, prioritized strategies (should only be three), and key outcomes
- Measure the impact of each assignment or project to determine the bigger to the lesser impact – start with the bigger impact first
- Understand the process time required to meet the deadline – to balance reality with hope and to negotiate with data
- Identify the key barriers to success and determine how much control you and your staff have
- Identify the key stakeholders who have control on the barriers that you and your staff have no control on
- Use the Eisenhower matrix of important and urgent – to prioritize your precious time on what matters

The Act of Subtracting

https://open.spotify.com/episode/4SN1UzjEN5PxKXPujN0h9e?si=g2y7vV6ZTNC4yWvvHVMYEg

ROLE & PRINCIPLES

Situational Leader-Manager Role

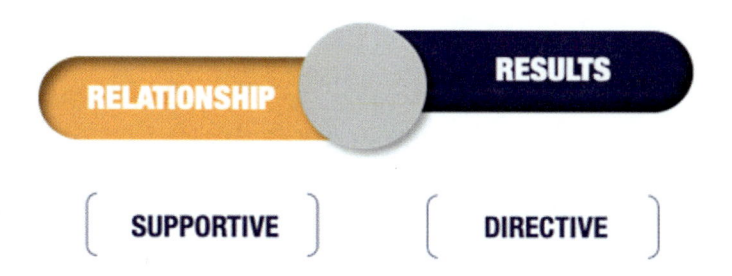

RELATIONSHIP | **RESULTS**

[SUPPORTIVE] [DIRECTIVE]

Leadership is about relationship requiring supportive behaviors, and management is about results requiring directive behaviors

Principles of Leadership

4P	4T
PRIVILIEGE	TRANSFORMATIONAL
PERSONAL	TRIALS & TRIBULATIONS
PERSONALIZED	TRAINING & DEVELOPMENT
PAINFUL	TRUISM

Teachable Points

✓ Connect before you are given permission to lead
✓ Build relationship based on mutual trust and respect which comes with time and actions
  o Not given but earned
✓ Great leaders are always learning
✓ Great leaders know when to ask for help
✓ Only fear and pride prevent learning
  o Courage and humility required

4P & 4T

https://open.spotify.com/episode/7dtkuy1T3D0YBGbAGTblW1?si=CwE0daqLSoCmPrSWFFQ6Bw

PRACTICE TWO

SITUATIONAL LEADER-MANAGER

Key Point: No One Style Is Appropriate For All Situations, Instead Choose From 4 Styles To Each Situation Balancing Supportive & Directive Behaviors For Relationship & Results

Why You Should Become A Leader-Manager

https://open.spotify.com/episode/4BQGI9daKjkNpPZgGdjvOA?si=93kM2C8rR3e7z4fLAlmRkg&context=spotify%3Ashow%3A0qewTFcM3EZIQOD9Lw89JK

Situational Leader-Manager Framework
*modified by Chin Teik

COACH Low – Moderate Directive High Supportive	**SUPPORT/SELL** Low Directive High Supportive
DELEGATE Low Directive Low Supportive	**TELL** High Directive Low Supportive

Supportive Behavior (y-axis)

Directive Behavior (x-axis)

D4	D3	D2	D1
High Capability High Commitment Current Role	High Capability High Commitment Current to Future Role	Moderate to High Capability Variable Commitment	Low Capability High Commitment

Principles of Situational Leadership

- Different Strokes for Different Folks
- Different Strokes for Same Folks
- Directive Behaviors to Build Competence
- Supportive Behaviors to Build Confidence and Engagement

Steps to Apply Situational Leader-Manager Framework

Step 1 Clarity for Focused Execution

Ensure the leader-manager is clear of the results (lag outcomes) expected and the mindset, capabilities and competencies required to carry out the tasks. More often than not, expectations are unclear as well as poorly communicated by the manager. It is important to communicate the 'why' and 'what' with the 'how'. It may be required to equip the employee to identify and focus on the leading indicators to the lag outcomes.

Step 2 Accurately Assess the Individual's Will and Way

Assess the current Will (drive and motive) with the Way (capabilities & competencies) of the employees and whether they are able to meet the expectations. If this is not carried out well, then the chances of a wrong leadership style being applied will be higher. This is also to clarify whether the employee is right for the role.

Step 3 Choose the Appropriate Leadership Style

Choose the appropriate leadership style to use with the specific employee and the specific situation. The 4 leadership styles to choose from are:

- **Tell/Teach/Instruct**
    - The style is characterized by one-way communication in which the leader defines the roles of the individual or group and provides the why, what, how, when and where to do the task
    - Teach before coach; when an employee is D1, the competence to do the job requires the leader-manager to teach and instruct on the 'how'.

- This style matches with new hires or newly promoted or internal transfers requiring an integration or transition. It might work with poor performers.

➤ **Support/Sell**
- The leader-manager is providing fewer task behaviors while maintaining high relationship behavior; increase in shared decision-making about aspects of task accomplishment.
- The leader-manager provides the right support to the follower's needs based on the situation including affirmation and recognition and/or help to remove barriers.
- With every new behavior required or a new goal to be achieved, the leader-manager will need to "sell" for the unfreezing of the brain (SCARF) against threats using the 5R. This style is intended to create buy-in and understanding.

➤ **Coach**
- The leader-manager coaches high performers to the next level of performance or to the next a broader or bigger roles; transfers perspective and network during this coaching process.
- My personal practice has been to set up coaching as an earned benefit for high-performing employees. My rule is to teach before you coach. The coaching style often goes hand-in-hand with delegating. When I am developing an identified successor, one of the developmental approaches is to provide coaching with the accompanying delegation.
- Do not use the coaching style for poor performers. You do not need to pause and understand the performance gap, the current situation and root cause to determine the solution and appropriate leadership style. This is also not life coaching.

- **Delegate**
    - The leader-manager delegates to high-performing employees who have obtained trust with their consistent performance and mastery over key capabilities and competencies, combined with intrinsic motivation that drives their commitment to excellence. This is to create an environment of autonomy for the high-performing employee with strong will.
    - The rule for delegating the work associated with the current role is a demonstration of 90% mastery. The rule for delegating to the next role is to identify one to two developmental areas.

'Help employees to discover their intrinsic motivation (Will) on work – current and new – and equipping them so that they can have autonomy on choice of how work gets done (Way).' – Chin Teik

Reflection for Insights (Aha!)

Observations, New Concepts Aha!	How does this apply to ME, my-TEAM & my-GROUP?	Actions to MYSELF What, When, How, Why

ELEMENT ONE

INDIVIDUAL BREAKTHROUGH PERFORMANCE

Breakthrough Performance

https://open.spotify.com/episode/0M62c6r28fkNl3MYdGsBnv?si=zLIhXTG4RduXKFfq_eFv5A

Individual Breakthrough Performance

Accountability is NOT responsibility

- Accountability is always at the individual level, NEVER at the organization, group or department level
- Accountability requires consequences for it to work at the individual level
- Accountability requires self-discipline
- Accountability requires a system and process because not every individual has self-discipline and self-drive

Individual Breakthrough Performance

Breakthrough Performance Habits	Role of Individual	Role of Leader-Manager
Executing on Leading Indicators to Achieve Lag Outcomes	• Ensure 100% clarity of lag outcomes • Translate into key leading indicators for focused execution	• Pause to think deeper • Be clear of outcomes (vs tasks) and lead indicators • Link to 3 prioritized strategies to achieve the vision – connect why to how • Assess Will & Way of individuals' 70:20:5

Visual Self-Monitoring Performance Feedback on Leading indicators (Output)	• Capability to design a reverse-engineered Gantt chart to track daily
	• Self-discipline and accountability
		• Discipline to run the weekly work preview – do not cancel
		   ○ Keep focus
		   ○ Hold accountability
		• Discipline to keep it to 1 minute
		• Discipline to NOT take over the problem

Control of Resources To Get Back on Track	• Pause to Re-Think on root cause and support required • Demonstrate the difference between what the individual controls and must act on versus what the individual cannot control and seek timely help • Demonstrate courage to provide "heads-up" and timely decision to deliver zero surprise	• Be ready to equip root cause problem solving so that the individual can own the solution • Be ready to support and/or connect to stakeholders who can provide support to the 95% of no control by the individual

Acknowledgment to William R. (Bill) Daniels for the Breakthrough Performance

The Power of Leading Indicators

Today, most organizations' focus is on lag indicators. My advice to them is don't, because lag indicators mean it is are **too late!** The principle is that data 24 hours late is useless because it is too late and often hard to make up for the gap.

While **a lag measure** tells you if you've achieved the goal, **a lead measure** tells you if you are likely to achieve the goal. A lead measure is a **predictive measurement**, for example, the number of calls made to potential clients in a given hour and the percent of closure. Lead measures allow you to shift the focus from the rear view perspective of "how did I do?" (1 month or 1 quarter or 1 year later) to the current and actionable view of "how am I doing?" (By the hour) that truly fuels execution. Lead measures are the highest leverage actions or activities that can accomplish goals. Lead measures can influence the chance of success in achieving your goal. Lag is too late!

Self-monitoring a lead measure provides data for action; getting back on track or asking for help to remove barriers.

The differences between the leading and lag indicators are that:

- leading indicator can influence change (get performance back on track)
- lagging indicator records what has happened

My observation in working with my client organizations is that lag indicators are easier to measure and are common. It does not take much effort to come up with the indicators. Leading indicators are always more challenging to determine and require deep and slow thinking.

However, it is worth the time and effort and is required for the individual breakthrough performance – Habit 1.

Examples

- Engaged and motivated employees are leading indicators of customer satisfaction
- Capable process (Six Sigma) is a leading indicator of cost efficiency (rework reduction and lead time reduction)
- Number of cold calls per day or percent of conversion per day are leading indicators to the revenue lag outcome
- Working out 3 times a week, on a low carb diet or 3 times a week intermittent fasting are leading indicators to weight management (lag outcome)

The Power of Leading Indicators
https://open.spotify.com/episode/5lLFasA18T2oValWORjyzh?si=Z2UAcF7oTPKFcg_hsrpnpg

Individual Breakthrough Performance Development Areas

The Neuroscience Approach: Will & Way of Setting & Achieving Goals

Source: Andrew Huberman

"**Will**" is the motive, a driving force, or reason for action taken. It can come from the benefits associated with the process of pursuing a goal — intrinsic motivation.

"**Way**" is the means to achieving a new goal, including skills, capacities & the knowledge.

70:20:5 Rule is the amount of time spent on utilizing an employee's strengths (70%), developing an employee (20%), and being mindful of the employee's weakness (5%).

- Strength is defined as high passion, high ability and should be used 70% of the time
- Development is defined as high passion, low ability and should take up 20% of the time at work
- Weakness is defined as low passion, low ability and should not spend more than 5% of the time because of low passion

Based on the above requirements, identify 70:20:5 of yourself, your staff, or team members in the table on next page.

Breakthrough Performance Elements & Capabilities	Individual	Leader-Manager
Executing on leading-to-lag outcomes Translating lag outcomes to leading indicators Success mindsets Growth, open, outward, promotion	70: 20: 5:	70: 20: 5:
Visual Self-Monitoring Performance Feedback via: • Reverse-engineered gantt chart • Self-discipline to self-monitor daily (dopamine reward) and act when off-track	70: 20: 5:	70: 20: 5:
Control of Resources • Discernment between control and no control • Structured problem solving ability • Stakeholder engagement ability • Courage to ask for help	70: 20: 5:	70: 20: 5:

Reflection for Insights (Aha!)

Observations, New Concepts Aha!	How does this apply to ME, my-TEAM & my-GROUP?	Actions to MYSELF What, When, How, Why

PRACTICE THREE

RHYTHM OF ACCOUNTABILITY

Keeping Performance on Track

Individual Reflection / Group Discussion

1. How do you monitor your people's performance?

2. What do you do when your staff's performance is not on track?

3. How well does each of your staff know their performance at any given moment in time?

2-Rhythm: Relationship-Accountability

Situational Leader-Manager Role

RELATIONSHIP — **RESULTS**

[SUPPORTIVE] [DIRECTIVE]

relationship
- ✓ 1x / month
- ✓ Employee engagement
- ✓ Performance alignment

accountability
- ✓ 1x / week
- ✓ Performance status to plan

The relationship meeting is between the employee and the leader-manager and is called one-on-one (1:1).
- It is regularly scheduled for once a month
- It is the employee's meeting and the agenda is set by the employee

- The employee sends the agenda 24 hours before the scheduled meeting in case of need to prepare like for questions on salary or compensation or promotion
- The leader-manager's role is to listen and support and not to take over the meeting
- The 1:1 is never cancelled to demonstrate the commitment to this relationship-rhythm

When I used to run 1:1s, I had a request that the last 10 minutes is set aside for mutual performance feedback and alignment.

The once-a-week rhythm of accountability is called 'weekly work preview' and is not called a weekly check-in. It is also not a weekly huddle because the huddle includes a group.

- The weekly work preview is around the individual's commitment to execute based on the reverse-engineered Gantt chart. It should be less than a minute.
- Given the breakthrough performance habit 2 – visual self-monitoring performance feedback – the employee should know exactly the status of the commitment. Therefore it is either '**on-track**' or '**not-on-track**'.
- If the status is not-on-track, the employee must demonstrate an effort to get back on track prior to scheduled meeting or know the root cause of not being able to get back on track.
- **Caution**. Be careful to not let the employee transfer the solution to the problem to you, the leader-manager. Have great self-discipline to not take over the problem because 'I know best' or 'We don't have time for me to teach you.'

Keeping Right Performance on Track

Reasons for keeping right performance on track

- At a personal level, we want to do a good job

- We all want to achieve the organization's goals to remain competitive and at the same share the reward of success

Do you agree with the above reasons?
Any other reasons to add?

Principles

- Data 24 hours late is useless – too late to make up
- All performances will, at some point, go off-track
- Humans are easily distracted — urgent over important
- Self-monitoring of performance provides immediate feedback (dopamine release)
- Data leads to choice of action

Do you agree with the above principles?

Reverse-Engineered Gantt Chart: Commitment to Execution & Rhythm of Accountability

To be used in the weekly work preview

Outcomes / Output	Process Time	Owners	Schedule
			○ Immediate quarter = workweeks ○ Next quarter = months ○ 12 months = quarters (Q1, Q2, Q3, Q4)
Output 1			
Output 2			
Output 3			
Project Y Implemented			March 15

1. Output 1 + output 2 + output 3 + output 4 + output 5 = 1 Outcome
    a. Output = leading indicator

2. Process time is a key variable to determine the confidence in the promise to meet the final outcome and target deadline
   - Available process time versus target process time to determine confidence level

3. Only one owner per output for accountability

4. Every output should have 2 rows for updating
   - Forecast process time
   - Actual process time accomplished

Objectives of Reverse-engineered Gantt chart
- To determine whether the project deadlines can be met during the mental creation (pre-plan)
   - Visual data to negotiate if the available process time cannot meet the deadline process time
- To build a detailed execution schedule with clear owner/output with process time commitment
   - Focusing on lead (predictor of success) and removal of barriers
- To keep the right performance on track with zero surprises

Keeping Right Performance on Track

Rhythm of Accountability - Weekly Work Preview

Given the principles from previous page, the weekly work preview is designed to:

- ➢ Make data as real time as possible
- ➢ Keep the employee focused and accountable
- ➢ Enable the employee to use the control of resources to get back on track

Process and Principles of Weekly Work Preview

Process	Role	Principles and Remarks
Communicate Clear Expectations of Assignment • Leading and lag outcomes • Behaviors • New competencies or capabilities	Leader-Manager	Humans are not intuitively clear in communication of expectations The human attention span is 9 seconds People tend not to seek clarification
Check for Understanding	Leader-Manager Employee	Assumption makes Ass-U-Me Guessing results in rework
Understand Goals, Milestones, and Schedule • Anticipate three barriers	Employee	Lag indicators are too late Leading indicators predict future success
Self-monitoring on daily basis Schedule dopamine release for "Will"	Employee	Self-discipline is not inherent in all individuals Self-monitoring leads to self-accountability and timely actions
Schedule fixed for weekly work preview of 2 minutes or less	Leader-Manager	This is the Leader-Manager's meeting It is never cancelled
Ground rules of process	Leader-Manager	People need to know what and how to behave in different situations Do not take over the problem

		Equip the employee

Keeping Right Performance on Track

Behaviors of Leader-Manager and Employee based on Performance Status — **"On Track or Not-on-Track"**

Performance Status	ROLE	
	Leader-Manager	**Employee**
Performance on Track	Provide Positive Feedback **SPPIFI**	Focus on keeping the rhythm
Performance Not on Track	1. Do not take over the problem; ask for barriers, or who is blocking or the root cause 2. Assess the capability and confidence of the employee to solve the problem 3a. Schedule a follow-up or 3b. Schedule a working session to teach employees structured problem-solving 3c. Schedule a session to provide coaching on stakeholder engagement Follow **Rules of Advice**	1. Do not surprise leader-manager 2. Be ready to share the barriers or root causes and to recommend actions to get back on track or the support required to get back on track

Reminder of Ground Rules to Teach to Each Staff
- Zero Surprise
- Timely Heads-Up (when performance is behind)
- Come with Solution to Problem

Reflection for Insights (Aha!)

Observations, New Concepts Aha!	How does this apply to ME, my-TEAM & my-GROUP?	Actions to MYSELF What, When, How, Why

PRACTICE FOUR

2 RULES OF FEEDBACK

If You Don't Show Appreciation To Those Who Deserve It, They'll Learn To Stop Doing The Things You Appreciate

Pause to Reflect

1. What is the goal or purpose of providing or receiving feedback?

2. What is the difference between "honest" and "meaningful" feedback?

3. How did you learn feedback? Can you remember when you first received feedback?

4. What types of feedback do you use on people? Do you use different feedback at home and at work?

Feedback Right

Feedback = Threat (to our brains)

- The brain wants to maximize reward and minimize threat
- Given that many of us have learned giving and receiving feedback in a non-structured approach but more of learning-from-experience, many of us have not had positive experiences with feedback
- Typically, our status (**self-worth**) and relatedness (**safety and connection-trust**) are impacted

Talent requires feedback to know whether he/she is on the right track. Feedback is intuitive and based on how each person has experienced from family, teachers and bosses. No one through functional degrees and higher level of education has learned structured feedback.

During the first 100-day of new hire integration, it is important for the change & transition process that each new hire knows in timely fashion whether he/she is on the right track in terms of learning, performance and fit to values and culture.

Feedback Right is designed around **two rules** ONLY:
- **Rule of Positive Feedback**
- **Rule of Advice**

I strongly encourage leader-managers to unlearn negative feedback because there is no upside but loads of downside. Negative feedback is not meaningful and leaves multiplier scars.

- The employee feels de-motivated by the negative feedback
- The employee does not know what to do with the negative feedback; when the feedback is ineffective, causing threat, the brain shuts down and does not hear
- The employee passes the negative feedback practice forward

Application of Principles

Principles	Time Frame	Types of Feedback
Right Talent wants to know what is required to meet expectations real time	Employee life cycle starts with interview and the first 90 days in office	• Role Expectations
Right Talent wants to know how they are doing in terms of performance	From First 100 days onwards	• Rules of Positive Feedback • Rules of Advice
Right Talent wants to develop and grow	From First 100 days onwards	• Rules of Positive Feedback • Rules of Advice

2 Rules of Feedback

Rules of Positive Feedback: SPPIFI
- **S**pecific
- **P**ure
- **P**ositive
- **I**mmediate
- **F**requent
- **I**nfrequent

Rules of Advice
- Current Behavior & Impact
- Get to Agreement
- Ask "Ready for Advice"
- Desired Behavior & Impact
- Assess Capability & Support Required

3 "C" to Assess Change-Able
- Commitment
- Capability
- Courage

Acknowledgment to William R. (Bill) Daniels for the 2 Rules of Feedback

Reflection for Insights (Aha!)

Observations, New Concepts Aha!	How does this apply to ME, my-TEAM & my-GROUP?	Actions to MYSELF What, When, How, Why

ELEMENT TWO

CULTURE OF EXECUTION

"A Culture Of Discipline Is Not A Principle Of Business, It Is A Principle Of Greatness" – Jim Collins, Good to Great

Culture To Be Taught Not Assumed

https://open.spotify.com/episode/5zVmv3Hd6Ozqxrup3FL2mZ?si=k6KHCDjDT7aC-DqHmsgMMA

Culture of Execution

Culture is the manifestation of values. **Values** are intrinsic for decision-making. Culture is extrinsic seen in an organization's management practices for execution. Culture, unlike values, differentiates and weeds out those who don't fit because poor practices can be seen.

Those practices are not soft skills but require frameworks, processes, and behaviors to be transferable, repeatable, and predictable.

1. How are your organization's values lived?
2. What is your organization's culture?
3. What are the prioritized practices required to achieve the organization's promise to its customers as well as achieve its vision?
4. How are new hires from a different culture **integrated** into the organization's culture?

Culture: What Do You Need To Work On?

No.	Practices	They Are Transferable, Repeatable, Predictable	Require Work Due To Lack of Structure and Process
1	Critical Thinking: 4 Key Questions The 2-Page		
2	Commitment to Execution via Reversed-Engineered Gantt Chart		
3	Structured Problem-Solving & Decision-Making		
4	Breakthrough Performance Three Habits		
5	Stakeholder Engagement & Communicating for Impact		
6	High Performing Teams		
7	Issue Clearing & Conflict Management		
8	2-Rhythm of Relationship & Accountability		
9	2-Rules of Feedback		

10	Change Leadership and Transition Management		
11	Talent Engagement Habits & System		
12	Performance Management Habits & System		
13	Customer Service Habits		
14	Effective Meetings		

Execution is not just tactics – it is a discipline of habits and systems.

Reflection for Insights (Aha!)

Observations, New Concepts Aha!	How does this apply to ME, my-TEAM & my-GROUP?	Actions to MYSELF What, When, How, Why

PRACTICE FIVE

CRITICAL THINKING VIA

2-PAGE TOOL

2-Page: Critical Thinking Documented

https://open.spotify.com/episode/4n9dUagRR2U9PDiagaweuC?si=YgrGPowdQCCnmUvZdvh0Hw

https://youtube.com/watch?v=7PeRm6gj_2w&feature=share

Critical Thinking via 2-Page

Critical thinking is asking the right questions. By asking the right questions, you can make informed decisions as objectively as you can from various sources of information. The required capabilities include questioning, listening to understand, interpretation, inference, reflection, problem-solving, solution discovery, and decision-making. Unfortunately, many leader-managers are not equipped with the capabilities described for critical thinking. Critical thinking requires System 2/refle**c**tive thinking (Think slow and deep). Due to the environment and biases, most leader-managers are using System 1/refle**x**ive thinking (Think fast and shallow). I have observed that from having taught this 2-Page to 1,000 executives.

Another challenge is that there is no editing function between our thoughts and our spoken words. Conciseness is clarity. Clarity is mastery in simplicity. **Thinking is writing**.

4 Key Questions: Make It an Organization Practice

A. What are you trying to solve?	Baseline	Perspective
B. How do you measure success?	Interpretation	Zero-Surprise
C. What are the three barriers to success?	Anticipation	Strategy to remove barriers
D. What support is required to remove these barriers	Stakeholder engagement 95% no control	Team members

50 : 30 : 20 Rule

4 Key Questions

50% of time to baseline
30% of time to interpret
20% of time for solution

Application of Problem/Gap Statement – Scope, Prioritization, Change

Start with the following elements:

Gap (Scope)
What is the difference between the: ➢ Current State ➢ Desired State
Impact of the Gap (Prioritization)
Which key indicator is being impacted and by how much?
Duration of the Gap (Change Management)
➢ How long has the gap been in existence? ➢ What are the challenges to achieve desired state?

Here is another way to frame the problem. Try it.

Problem Statement		
Current State - Quantify		
Desired State - Quantify		
Gap Difference between current and desired state	**Impact of the Gap** Business Indicator Impacted	**Duration of the Gap** How long has the gap been around?

Reflection for Insights (Aha!)

Observations, New Concepts Aha!	How does this apply to ME, my-TEAM & my-GROUP?	Actions to MYSELF What, When, How, Why

PRACTICE SIX

STRUCTURED PROBLEM-SOLVING

Structured Problem-Solving

At this point, I would like to introduce the **structured problem-solving** methodology, which will help in answering the **4 questions** as well as help in closing the root cause gaps in the project implementation.

Key to problem-solving is to **fix the root cause,** not the symptom!

➢ **Symptom** is what you see – iceberg model. 'I am overweight' is a symptom. A symptom approach is to wear bigger size clothes.

➢ **Root cause** is typically hidden – iceberg model. When you ask **5-why**, you will probably get to the root cause. Ask a series of questions starting with 'Why am I overweight?'

> A series of root cause solutions will be:
> o regular exercise
> o balanced diet
> o regular sleeping hours

Structured problem solving is made up of **7 steps** and relies on data and observations to solve problems.

The advantages of using the structured problem-solving include:

✓ Common language and methodology for project team members to baseline and interpret effectively – 50:30:20 Rule
✓ Delivers repeatable and predictable results

The 7 steps are:

1. **Define Problem Statement**
2. **Current Situation Analysis**
3. **Root Cause Analysis**
4. **Develop Solution**
5. **Implement Solution**
6. **Standardize**
7. **Next Steps**

You will notice that step 1 of structured problem solving is the same as question A of the 2 Page. It is not by accident.

Einstein has been quoted to say that if he had only 60 minutes to save the world, he would spend 59 minutes figuring out the problem and 1 minute to solve it.

Effective teams spend around 80% of project time on baseline and interpretation and only 20% on developing solutions.

Therefore, when you do not get step 1: "Define the Problem Statement," right, the rest of the steps will be a waste of time.

> Please note the synthesis between the 4 questions and the 7 steps of structured problem solving on the next page. You will observe that **3 out of the 5 steps revolve around baseline and interpret** so that paradigms and assumptions are dealt with as early as possible in the process.

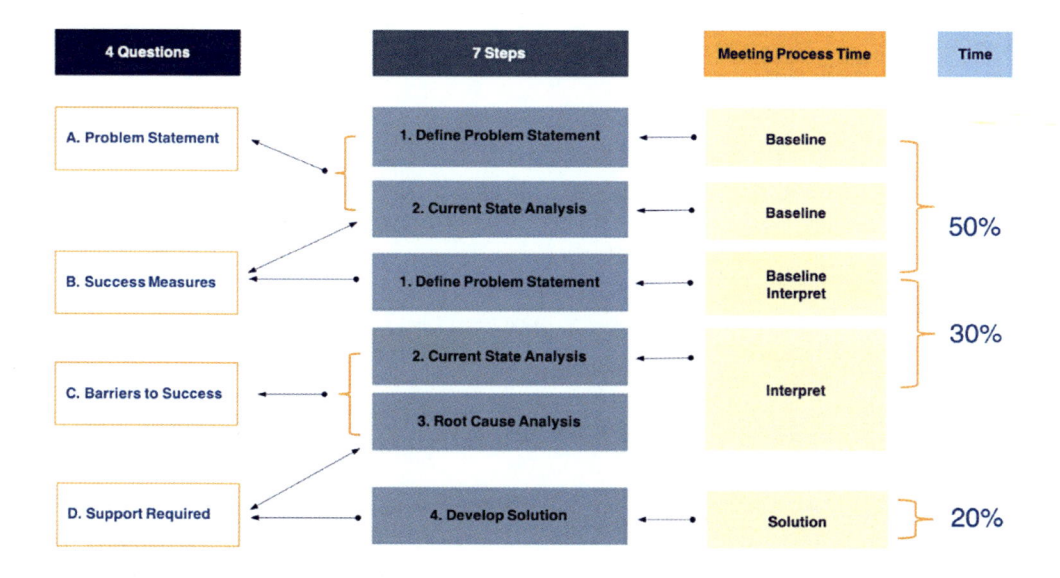

4 Questions	7 Steps	Meeting Process Time	Time
A. Problem Statement	1. Define Problem Statement	Baseline	
	2. Current State Analysis	Baseline	50%
B. Success Measures	1. Define Problem Statement	Baseline Interpret	
	2. Current State Analysis	Interpret	30%
C. Barriers to Success	3. Root Cause Analysis		
D. Support Required	4. Develop Solution	Solution	20%

50:30:20 Rule

"If I had an hour to solve a problem, I'd spend 55 minutes thinking about the problem and 5 minutes thinking about the solution."

"We cannot solve our problems with the same level of thinking that created them." ~ Albert Einstein

1. Define Problem Statement

Current state and goals agreed to (gap is clear)
Impact of the gap to th business agreed to (specific and measurable)
Duration of the gap is clear and agreed to (how long has the identified gap been around?}
Problem statement will be confirmed after step 3 (root cause analysis) before step 4 (develop solution)

❖ **Use Data as much as possible**

2. Current Situation Analysis

> ➤ All team members understand the current state (100% base lined)
> - o Current state helps to understand root cause and/or barriers
>
> ➤ Current state is documented on process flow or
> - o Value and non-value steps (checking, decision-making points) are identified
> - o Recommend that members walk to the area of the problem to see for themselves the current state
>
> ➤ Team members use data to understand current situation
> - o Use data to look for trends – 7 data points make a trend

A Picture Paints A Thousand Words

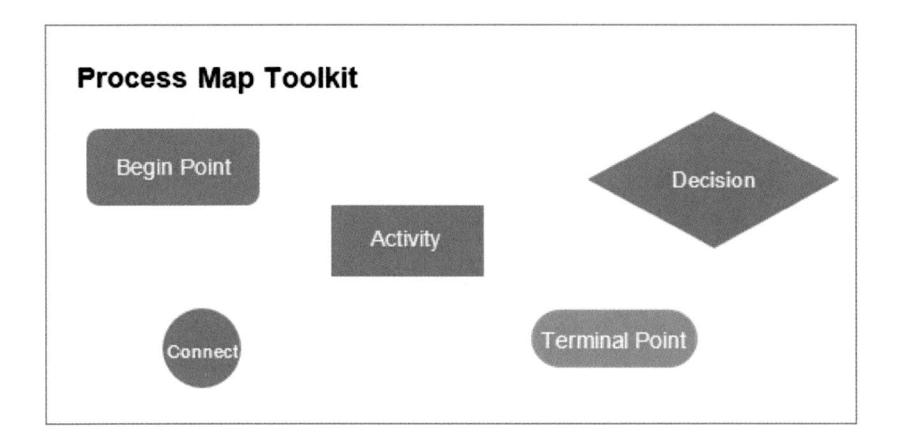

```
Process Map Toolkit

  [Begin Point]                    ◆ Decision
              [ Activity ]
  (Connect)              (Terminal Point)
```

1. **The more detailed the process map is, the more effective the team will be in understanding gaps and opportunities in the current state and root cause analysis.**

    ➢ A visible documented process map enables re-thinking of the current state by clearing the curtain on blind spots
    ➢ Do not **assume** that everyone sees the same thing (SEEDS)
    ➢ SOP is not a detailed process map of current state; it is a summarized version of ideal state, which may not have been operationalized

2. **Recommend that team members spend time walking to the area where the 'problem' is.**

3. **Use as much data as available.**

Process Map – Visual Data on Current State
Practice drawing a process map using the icons shared on previous page

3. Root Cause Analysis

- Fishbone (Ishikawa) diagram used effectively (as many sub-bones as possible) to identify root cause
    - Positive fishbone
    - Negative fishbone

- Dump & clump process used (everyone has equal influence – think 'Hill of Influence') with brainwriting

- Top 3 root causes identified

- Ask 5-why to get to the root cause
    - The more sub-bones, the clearer the root cause

- The team has verified the root cause with data

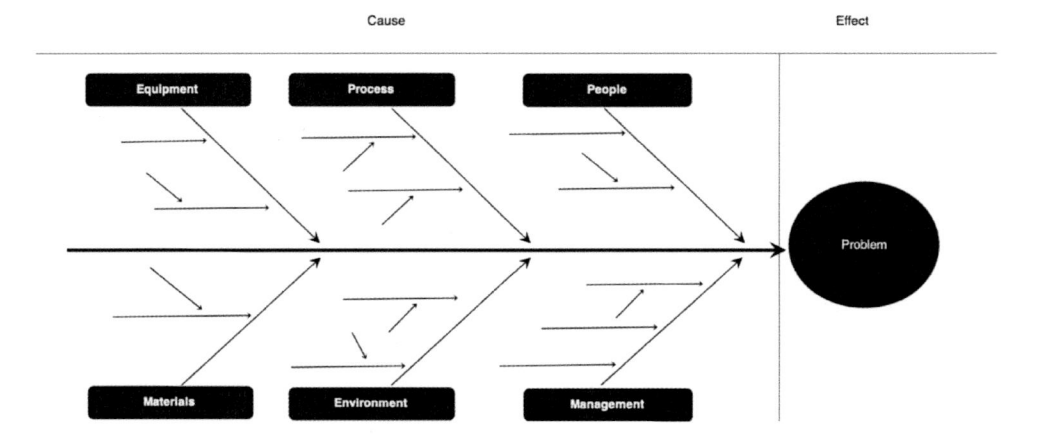

The above diagram is just an example of how Dr. Ishikawa used the fishbone diagram in the 1960s to pioneer quality management processes in the Kawasaki shipyard.

The basic concept was first used in the 1920s, and is considered one of the seven basic tools of quality control.

In the manufacturing world, the 5Ms will be used for the causes including:

- **M**achine
- **M**ethod
- **M**an
- **M**aterial
- **M**easurement

In the marketing industry, either the 4 Ps or 7 Ps can be used, including:

- **P**roduct/service
- **P**romotion
- **P**rice
- **P**lace

And 7Ps with the addition of:

- **P**eople
- **P**rocess
- **P**hysical evidence

With the brainstorming - dump and clump - process, we don't necessarily have to start with a pre-determined 5M or 4P or 7P. The process will allow the team to clump the categories from the brainstorming effort.

Recommended Dump & Clump Process for Brainstorming

The **"Dump and Clump"** process is designed to include 100% of team members' engagement. Group wisdom begins with individual creativity.

Dump and Clump Process uses Brainwriting

This inclusive process works well especially in an Asian environment because of the 'content over form' mental model of most Asians. The traditional brainstorming requires the facilitator to go around asking team members for ideas. The team member can say 'pass' if he/she has no idea. Due to conformity pressure, noise, and status threat, good ideas are lost; not everyone's voice is heard.

My observation on the traditional brainstorming is that the pressure to think on the spot is very stressful for many folks who are trained to be more content than form focused or due to language constraint.

I find the Dump and Clump process allows everyone to think ahead together before speaking. This will also neutralize the dominant team member or the team member who can speak/think on the spot quickly.

The Dump and Clump process:

- Everyone is given 2 minutes to write down as many ideas as possible
    - one idea on one post-it
- During the 2 minutes, a facilitator takes completed post-its and **dumps** them onto a flipchart
- After the 2 minutes, everyone stops writing down ideas
    - Everyone stands up and gathers around the flipchart and helps with the dump
- The facilitator now reminds everyone that it is time for the sharing of ideas and the ground rules
- When the facilitator picks up a post-it, whoever is the owner of the post-it, will share the idea
- During the sharing, the rules are to listen and not to interrupt
    - All ideas are good ideas
    - Piggyback on other's ideas
- During the sharing of ideas, the team will start to **clump** common ideas and themes
- At the end of the sharing, everyone will spend time to agree on the key root causes

#TIPS for you

Tip #1: Drill down the sub-bones to get to root cause

- Dr. Ishikawa recommended that the more you can drill down (example: **asking 5-WHY**), the higher the chances you will get to the root cause.

Tip #2: The first bone is usually the symptom

- Please don't stop there.
- You will be wasting your resources fixing symptoms rather than root causes.

Tip #3: Know what you can control

- There are some root causes that will be out of the team's control.
- Know what those root causes are and whether there are internal forces that can help to remove them.

Tip #4: Do not oversimplify to power point - Miss the narrative

- Show the workings from the flipchart in terms of the fishbone with the post-its (principle behind **Design Thinking**).
- Without seeing the 5-Why from symptom to root cause, your key stakeholders' paradigms will not shift.

Fishbone Diagram | Root Cause Analysis
Practice drawing a fish bone diagram and asking 5 Why

4. Develop Solution – System Solution

1. System Solution approach includes
   - **Leadership**
   - **System includes**
     - Process
     - Policies
     - Tools
     - Structure
   - **People includes**
     - Mindset, Character, Capabilities, and Competencies
     - Right match to role

2. Each project team member must have influence on the actions committed for solution

3. Each action item has clarity on 4W & 1H:
   - Who (individual name not department)
   - What
   - How
   - When (specific date and month not Q1 or end of month)
   - Why

4. Sponsor or Mentor or Coach is effectively utilized
   - Areas of Control
   - Areas of No Control

System Solution

> I developed the **"System Solution"** and use it as the core of my neuroleadership coaching and consulting based on the following principles:
> - 90% of work problems come from systems designed by people (managers)
> - Organization change starts with the leader
> - Middle management has the hardest role in change management as they are caught in between
> - Structure influences behavior
> - Hiring right is the key to talent engagement system; the right talent does not need to be motivated – inspire, recognize, reward
> - Direct manager has a higher impact on the employees' behaviors
> - Action speaks louder than words

To implement a solution which usually requires change, the **"leadership"** box is the starting point. How willing is the leadership to change and to walk the talk, including changing behaviors, policies, procedures, and systems?

The **"system"** box is the one where the principle of "structure influences behavior" occurs. Put in place the right people with the right support and the permission to change what is not working. It is also the principle of designing the right system, policies, structure, and tools to shape and reinforce the desired behaviors.

An example is the **Talent Engagement System** designed for client organizations.

| #1 Hire Right | #2 Pay Right | #3 Integrate Right | #4 Feedback Right | #5 Train Right | #6 Develop Right |

The "people" box is the last box to work on. When leader-managers are walking the talk and the systems are designed to reinforce the right habits or to deliver capable processes to meet customer promise, the people will follow. The "people" box is about having the right people on the right bus.

System Solution: Change and Transformation Process

Leadership Behaviours	System	People Behaviours

Personal	Strategic Planning	Fit
Team	Talent Management	Fruitfulness
Department	Recognition	Engaged
Organization	Reward	Nimble & Resilience
	Work and Process Capable	
	Change & Transition	

Principles:

- Culture is visible via the leadership actions not words
- Change is inside out; help to discover the Will
- System contributes 90% to work problems
- 'Hire for Fit' is the critical success factor for talent engagement system
- Lead scalable change from leadership box
- Right structure influences right behavior

System Solution

Leadership	System	People

Reverse-Engineered Gantt Chart: Commitment to Execution & Rhythm of Accountability

Outcomes Output	Process Time	Owner	Schedule — Immediate quarter = workweeks; Next quarter = months; 12 months = quarters (Q1, Q2, Q3, Q4)
Output 1			March 15
Output 2			
Output 3			
Project Y Implemented			x

The reverse-engineered Gantt chart serves two objectives.

1st Objective: To ascertain whether the project deadlines can be met during the mental creation (pre-plan)

- When the available process time shows that the target deadline cannot be met during the pre-planning stage, you can negotiate with the sponsor or the manager

2nd Objective: To use the Gantt chart with the project team members to build a detailed implementation schedule

- Begin with the **measurable end-in-mind** where "**x**" marks the deadline and final outcome (row 7)
- Work backward and determine the output (**not tasks**) that need to be completed before project Y can be implemented
- One owner (only) per output for individual accountability
- Ensure the removal of barriers are reflected as output

Example:

Set up meetings with key stakeholder for go/no go' is a task.

Go/no-go decision made by key stakeholder by September 15 is an output.

For each output, determine the process time required. Add up the process time in the bottom row and see if the deadline process time can be met.

Example:

If the deadline is March 15 and the current date is January 14, then the total time is 8 working weeks and 3 days.

However, if the total process time to complete all the output is greater than 8 working weeks and 3 days, immediately the project deadline is a no-go.

This calls for negotiation on the deadline.

Owners need to sign up and commit to their output and agree on following behaviors:

- Self-monitor individual performance and ensure output can be met
- Gantt chart need to be visually displayed to serve as reminder (out of sight, out of mind) – public accountability
- Attend regular weekly work previews and provide quick update on status
- On track or not on track
    - If not on track, employees will have to share what is the barrier and support required

5. Implement Solution

- Visible self-monitoring gantt chart – public accountability
    - Visible
    - Well utilized by team to meet project goals

- Rhythm of Accountability being carried out

Weekly Work Preview	✓ On track or not on track

- Team members are:
    - Communicating effectively with impacted stakeholders
    - Zero surprise to stakeholders

- The team members are:
    - Regularly meeting face-to-face
    - It is to keep performance on track of implementation

- Team members are:
    - Able to deal with unforeseen barriers during implementation effectively

6. Standardize BKM (Better Known Method)

- Team members are still monitoring the implementation (1 to 3 months after implementation)
- Team members are regularly updating their stakeholders on solution status
- Better-Known-Methods (BKM) identified and documented
- Post-mortem on project implementation completed and communicated with coach/mentor/sponsor

7. Next Steps

- Post-mortem on solution status 2 to 3 months after implementation (level of adoption of solution)
- Key learning documented and shared with key stakeholders
- Closure for project team completed (including appropriate celebration and acknowledgement)
    - Inputs on each team member's contribution and participation provided to bosses of team members
- Better-Known-Method (BKM) agreed to, documented and adopted

Reflection for Insights (Aha!)

Observations, New Concepts Aha!	How does this apply to ME, my-TEAM & my-GROUP?	Actions to MYSELF What, When, How, Why

PRACTICE SEVEN

HIGH PERFORMING TEAMS

Facilitate High Performing Teams for Results

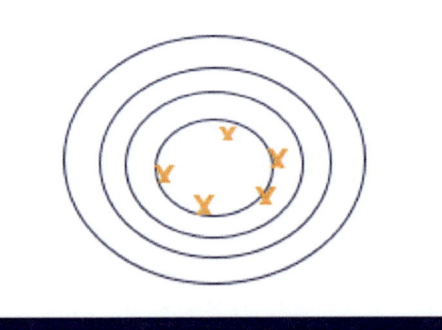

Hill of Influence
Mission Meeting Dynamics: equal influence

Tuckman Team Development
Forming/Reforming → Storming → Normin → Performing

Mission Meeting Effective Use of Time Methodology

Structured Problem-Solving

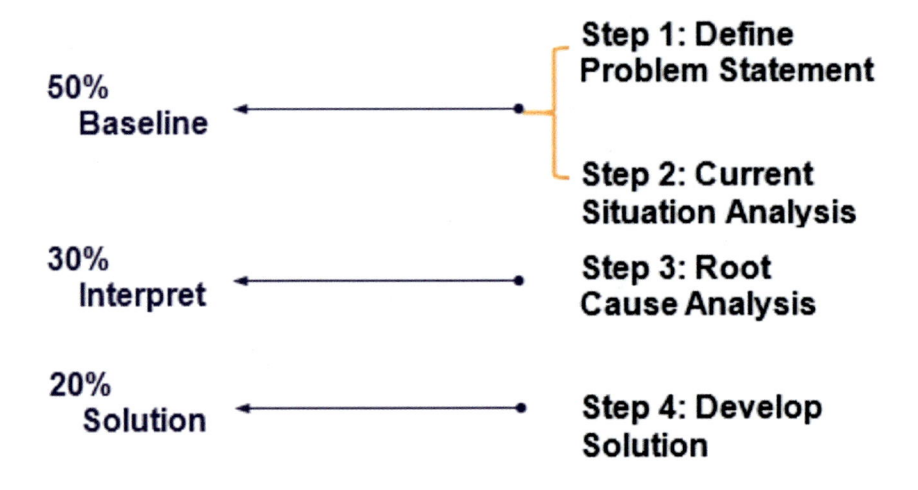

50% Baseline ← Step 1: Define Problem Statement
           ← Step 2: Current Situation Analysis

30% Interpret ← Step 3: Root Cause Analysis

20% Solution ← Step 4: Develop Solution

Characteristics of High Performing Team

✓ Everyone agrees and works on one common goal (shared group goal higher than individual goal)
✓ Everyone agrees and follows ground rules for team performance (fanatic discipline)
✓ Everyone is clear of his/her role and contribution (equal influence and engagement)
✓ Everyone agrees to use common tools and language for effectiveness (fanatic discipline)
✓ Everyone is an expert in his/her area (engagement)
✓ Data is used whenever possible (data driven, empirical creativity)
✓ Team meets regularly to work together (rehearsals, team development) to build rhythm of relationship and rhythm of accountability

Author's note: These are some of the tools that are used to facilitate a high-performing team for results

Criteria for High-Performing Team

1. Team membership

Criteria for Mission Team Membership:

- ➢ Part of problem
- ➢ Part of solution – those who will be implementing/owning the solution
- ➢ Expertise or experience in the problem/solution

Do not sacrifice effectiveness for over-inclusiveness

Inclusiveness without role accountability increases complexity and slows down decision-making (counterintuitive)

2. Size of Mission Team (core):

5, 7, or 9 team members, including team leader

#Note 1:

Keeping core team size small makes it easier to co-ordinate working sessions and follow-up

#Note 2:

The bigger your core team, the higher likelihood that someone will not be engaged and it will also slow down decision-making

#Note 3:

You can have sub-teams who do not join the core team working sessions

Process for Forming Team

Forming stage is key to setting up any new team for success.

- ❑ Obtain Buy-In: identified team member and his/her direct manager using 2-Page
- ❑ Face-to-Face session for first few times: human connection
- ❑ Breaking the Ice: Sharing to show complementary 70:20:5
- ❑ Setting Ground Rules: DEI – Diversity, Equity and Inclusion
- ❑ Clarifying Roles & Output/Outcome

Caution

Based on the 6 paradigms of human relationships, not everyone is programmed in their mindset to collaborate and go for a win-win.

- Win-win
- Win-lose
- Lose-win
- Lose-lose
- Win
- Win or no deal

No department simply becomes a team.

Reflection for Insights (Aha!)

Observations, New Concepts Aha!	How does this apply to ME, my-TEAM & my-GROUP?	Actions to MYSELF What, When, How, Why

PRACTICE EIGHT

STAKEHOLDER ENGAGEMENT

Mindset for Stakeholder Engagement

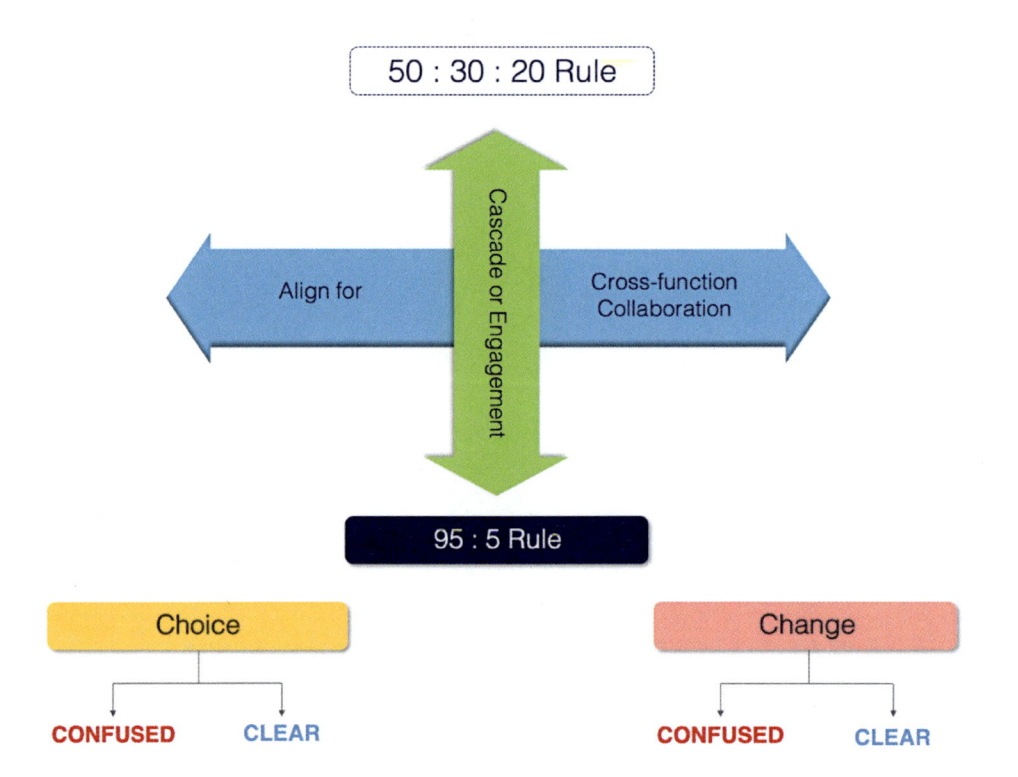

50 : 30 : 20 Rule

Cascade or Engagement

Align for ← → Cross-function Collaboration

95 : 5 Rule

Choice
- CONFUSED
- CLEAR

Change
- CONFUSED
- CLEAR

Stakeholder Analysis Template

Name	Importance Low/Medium/High	Relationship Low/Medium/High	Gap	Strategy	Support Required

Reflection for Insights (Aha!)

Observations, New Concepts Aha!	How does this apply to ME, my-TEAM & my-GROUP?	Actions to MYSELF What, When, How, Why

About The Book: Keeping Right Performance on Track

Execution requires a discipline of habits and system.

"Execution is the real differentiator in business." ~ Gary Hamel

"Execution without a strategy is aimless, strategy without execution is useless." ~ Morris Chang

"To me, ideas are worth nothing unless executed. They are just multiplier. Execution is worth millions." ~ Steve Jobs

In this how-to book toolkit, **'System of Execution—Keeping Right Performance on Track'**, you will learn and apply the framework, which has one requirement and two elements—**Disciplined Leadership, Individual Breakthrough Performance** and **Culture of Execution.**

The framework, tools, and methodologies with accompanying podcasts come from Chin Teik's personal and professional experiences and his use of the **neuroscience** learning pathway to provide **structured, simple, and practical tools** for **immediate application.** This toolkit is designed to be brain-friendly for recall under pressure and change with the reflection journal and the application practices. **Reflection to generate insights** as insights lead to action and change. This how-to book, when applied right will shift the mindset from commitment to plan to **commitment to execute.**

"Vision without execution is just hallucination." ~ Henry Ford

CHIN TEIK CONSULTING LTD

Offers: Greatness Series - Execution Series - Life Skills Series
Process Consulting - Senior Executive NeuroLeadership Coaching - Podcast Series
– YouTube series

CHIN TEIK CONSULTING LTD

SYSTEM OF EXECUTION
KEEPING RIGHT PERFORMANCE ON-TRACK

About Chin Teik

Chin Teik is a senior executive neuroleadership coach, an action-learning facilitator and a business/process consultant. He is an adjunct professor with the School of Education, at Taylor's University, Malaysia. Chin Teik's Why is 'To make an immediate and multiplier impact on people I care about and work with.' Chin Teik's vision is equipping leaders and managers with the understanding of the brain to make organizations more human in terms of leading scalable change, solving complex problems and decision-making in achieving business results. Chin Teik designs his own action-learning coaching and workshops based on the neuroscience learning pathway to make the sessions and interactions brain-friendly for recall and change. Chin Teik's clients cut across a variety of industries from advertising, private education, steel, F&B, life-style, public utilities, automotive body part manufacturing, on-line job portal, sports-wear and equipment, apparel accessories, banking, pharmaceutical and investment. In his 28 years with Intel, Chin Teik has facilitated/led 3 organizational transformations and co-founded one non-profit training center.

CHIN TEIK

Chin Teik Consulting Ltd